SPACE ACADEMY

How to fly spacecraft step by step

To the early prophets of space travel who in 1933 formed the British Interplanetary Society, the world's oldest rocket club for professionals, enthusiasts and young people everywhere – and still going strong!

First published in the United Kingdom in 2013 by Thames & Hudson Ltd, 181A High Holborn, London WC1V 7QX

Space Academy © 2013 Thames & Hudson Ltd, London

Created by picnic
Editorial Deborah Kespert
Design Belinda Webster

Text
Dr David Baker and Deborah Kespert

British Library Cataloguing-in-Publication Data
A catalogue record for this book is available from the British Library
ISBN 978-0-500-65014-1

Printed and bound in China by Toppan Leefung

To find out about all our publications, please visit **www.thamesandhudson.com**. There you can subscribe to our e-newsletter, browse or download our current catalogue, and buy any titles that are in print.

Illustrations
Black-and-white illustrations by Damien Weighill
Colour illustrations by Katharina Rocksien

On the cover
Front and back: above, stars (Clearviewstock/Dreamstime); below, Earth (Steve Bloom Images/Alamy); below, Phobos (NASA/JPL/University of Arizona). Illustrations by Belinda Webster. Front only: above left, rocket (courtesy Arianespace); above right, Moon (NASA); centre, Skylon (Courtesy REL/Adrian Mann); back only: above left, rocket (Courtesy ULA).

Photography credit
a = above, b = below, c = centre, l = left, r = right, bgd = background
Alamy AF Archive 7bl, 7br, 37bl, Steve Bloom Images 2–3b bgd, 10–11b, 16b, 18–19b, 24–25b, ITAR-TASS Photo Agency 7bc; Arianespace 36al; CSA 38c; Corbis 45c, Justin Dernier/epa 9bl, NASA/Roger Ressmeyer 31ar, Gary I. Rothstein/epa 37r; Dreamstime Balefire9 5ar, 7ar bgd, 9a bgd, 13a bgd, 35br bgd, Clearviewstock 2–3a bgd, 4–5 bgd, 6–7a bgd, 8–9a bgd, 10–11a bgd, 12–13a bgd, 14–15bgd, 16-17a bgd, 18–19a bgd, 20a bgd, 22–23, 24–25a bgd, 26–27bgd, 30–31bgd, 32–33a bgd, Jahoo 18–19bgd, 28–29a, Pitris 34–35bgd, 46–47bgd, Laurence Romaric 6l bgd, 8l bgd, 12l bgd, 20bl bgd, Junichi Shimazaki 35b; ESA 39c; Fotolia.com deviantART 17br bgd, jeremyculpdesign 26br; Intelsat 39al; Vitaly Korotkov 42l; Courtesy Petar Miloševic 44c; NASA 2, 3a, 4al, 5br, 5bl, 6r, 9bc, 9br, 10r, 12c, 13c, 14bl, 14ar, 14br, 15ar, 15cr, 17bl, 18r, 19b, 20bl, 21, 22cl, 22ar, 22bl, 23al, 23ar, 24r, 25al, 25ar, 26a bgd, 26cl 26cr, 27cla, 27cra, 27br, 30l, 30br, 30ar, 30al, 32a, 34a, 35a, 35c, 36l, 36c, 40l, 40c, 40r, 41al, 41ac, 41r, 42c, 42r, 43al, 43bl, 43c, 43r, 44l, 44r, 45r, JPL 27ar, 45al, JPL-Caltech 18bc, 28r, JPL-Caltech/MSSS 19bl, 29bl, JPL/Cornell 18–19b, 28–29b, JPL/University of Arizona 4bl, JPL/USGS 26ar, JSC 6–7b bgd, 8–9b bgd, 12–13b bgd, 14–15b bgd, 15al, 16r, 17br, NOAA GOES Project 39bl, NSSDC 38l, Kim Shiflett 41bl; REL/Adrian Mann 5c, 34b; Science Photo Library Chris Butler 27cr, NASA 45bl; ULA 36r, 37c, 39r; US Air Force 3b, 4br, 33br, 33bl, 38r; Virgin Galactic 32cr, 32cl

SPACE ACADEMY

How to fly spacecraft step by step

Deborah Kespert & David Baker

Thames & Hudson

YOUR SPACE ACADE

Are you ready to sign up to Space Academy?
Check out your timetable and blast off!

BE AN ASTRONAUT | 6

ROCKET POWER | 8

WE HAVE LIFT-OFF! | 10

MOON MISSION | 12

MOON LANDING | 14

BACK TO EARTH | 16

SHUTTLE LAUNCH | 18

SPACE STATION | 20

SPACEWALK | 22

Would you like to fly to the Moon or explore distant planets?

X-37B

X-37

NASA

BOEING

MY TIMETABLE

Are you ready to take a space shuttle into orbit?

Look out for these badges at the top of the page. They'll tell you whether you're studying in the classroom at astronaut school or on a live mission in space. Just like a professional astronaut, you'll learn everything step by step.

ASTRONAUT SCHOOL

BE AN ASTRONAUT

Before you can fly to the Moon or a space station, you need to train to be an astronaut. You'll study hard, practise all the things you'll do in space and get fit for your mission.

YOUR SPACESUIT

Let's begin by getting to know the most important piece of equipment – your spacesuit. This will keep you alive and help you to do jobs outside the spacecraft.

Camera
A camera takes pictures of what you're doing so other crew members can see too.

Visor
A gold visor shields your eyes from glaring sunlight.

Gloves
Flexible gloves let your fingers bend to help you carry out tasks.

Controls
Controls for heating and cooling the suit are on the chest pack in easy reach. Space is very cold!

Outer layer
A tough outer layer protects your body from sharp space particles, such as grains of sand, which can hit you at high speed. In space there is less friction to slow down moving objects.

Backpack
Oxygen is stored in the backpack and piped into your helmet. Space is almost totally empty – there's no air, so you can't breathe.

Jet pack
Astronauts wear rocket-powered jet packs to use in an emergency if separated from the spacecraft. Without gravity you are weightless, and could float away!

CHECKLIST!

To receive your official astronaut badge, you must complete these tasks:

✔ Learn how to fly an aeroplane and use the ejection seat.

✔ Go on an outdoor survival course to build up your mental strength.

✔ Practise dealing with emergencies.

✔ Pass a set of exams and perform a successful space flight.

TRAINING TIME

Most of your training takes place in conditions similar to space so that you are well prepared for your galactic experience. Get ready to ...

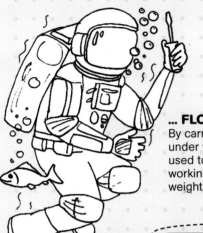

... FLOAT IN A TANK

By carrying out jobs under water, you'll get used to the idea of working while feeling weightless.

... FLY A SIMULATOR

Astronauts practise flying their spacecraft in a simulator, which looks just like a real flight deck. You can get simulator games on the computer.

... RIDE THE 'VOMIT COMET'

'Vomit Comet' is the nickname for a plane that lets an astronaut experience what it is like to float weightless in space. It might make you feel sick!

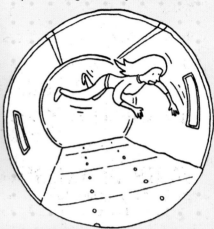

ASTRONAUT HEROES

Will these heroic astronauts inspire you to become a space traveller of the future?

YURI GAGARIN

In 1961, Soviet astronaut Yuri Gagarin became the first human to circle (orbit) the Earth. He spent nearly two hours travelling through space in his spacecraft Vostok 1 before returning safely.

VALENTINA TERESHKOVA

The first woman in space was also a Soviet. In 1963, inside Vostok 6, Valentina Tereshkova orbited the Earth 48 times for almost three days. She returned home a hero.

NEIL ARMSTRONG

In 1969, American astronaut Neil Armstrong became the first person to set foot on the Moon. People on Earth heard him say, 'That's one small step for (a) man, one giant leap for mankind.'

ROCKET POWER

You'll take your first trip to space in a rocket, so let's find out how one works. This is the Saturn V – the tallest, heaviest and most powerful rocket ever built!

SATURN V PARTS

Saturn V launched astronauts to the Moon on six separate missions between 1969 and 1972. Like most space rockets, it was made up of different sections, called stages, with a payload, or cargo, at the top. Each stage had its own engines and fuel. They fall away once they are used up.

ROCKET JOBS

A space rocket is a launch vehicle. It does all kinds of jobs, including …

✓ transporting astronauts.

✓ delivering parts to space stations.

✓ putting communication and weather satellites into orbit.

✓ launching space probes and space telescopes.

111 m

PAYLOAD
Saturn V's payload was a spacecraft. The astronauts travelled inside the spacecraft.

86 m

STAGE 3
The third stage of the rocket gave an extra push to send the astronauts towards the Moon.

68 m

STAGE 2
This second stage blasted the astronauts through the Earth's atmosphere – the layers of gas that surround our planet. After the atmosphere comes space!

43 m

STAGE 1
The first stage was the tallest and heaviest. It was powerful enough to lift the massive rocket off the ground.

How does a rocket get off the ground?

To take off, a rocket has to work against gravity, the force that pulls objects to Earth.

gravity

rushing gases cause a reaction – thrust

rocket lifts off

Inside a rocket engine, hot gases are produced by burning fuel. The gases rush out at high speed towards the ground, causing a reaction. This moves the rocket in the opposite direction towards space.

What fuel does a rocket burn?

A rocket burns solid fuel (a flammable powder) or liquid fuel, and sometimes both. Oxygen is needed to make the liquid fuel burn. This Ariane rocket, which is still in use, carries liquid fuel in the main tank and solid fuel in its boosters.

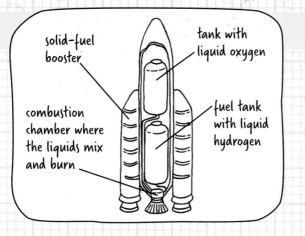

solid-fuel booster

tank with liquid oxygen

combustion chamber where the liquids mix and burn

fuel tank with liquid hydrogen

☞ Robert Goddard invented the first liquid-fuel rocket in 1926. It flew for two-and-a-half seconds to a height of 12 m, then landed in a cabbage patch.

☞ In the first two-and-a-half minutes after lift-off, Saturn V burned enough liquid fuel to nearly fill an Olympic swimming pool!

QUICK QUIZ

See if you can answer the questions by looking at the photos.

Where are the solid-fuel boosters on this Atlas V rocket?

Four solid-fuel boosters are strapped to the outside of the central stage. They provide extra thrust at lift-off.

Which stage of the Saturn V rocket are you looking at?

The first and largest stage. At the bottom, Saturn V has five powerful engines to lift it off the ground.

How is this Russian Soyuz rocket being moved to the launch pad?

Soyuz is pulled flat along a railway track by a train. Saturn V travelled upright on a motorised crawler with caterpillar tracks.

9

WE HAVE LIFT-OFF!

In 1969, during the Apollo 11 mission, US astronauts made history when they became the first humans to fly to the Moon and bounce across its dry, dusty surface. Get ready to lift off on your own Moon mission.

Head to the launch pad
You'll go to the Moon with two other astronauts inside a cramped Apollo spacecraft. The Apollo is perched on top of a massive Saturn V rocket that will blast you into space.

Did you know?
At 111 m, the Saturn V rocket stood higher than London's Big Ben! That's about 11 buses standing end to end.

1 The tower
The launch tower is 120 m high. Inside, a lift takes you up to Level 9 where you board the spacecraft.

2 The white room
A small white chamber at the end of a mechanical arm connects you to the spacecraft. At launch, the arm swings away.

3 Apollo spacecraft
The Apollo spacecraft is divided into different sections. The cone-shaped part where you sit is called the command module.

4 Engine power
At lift-off, the rocket engines will fire. The heat they give off is so fierce that it can melt the launch pad!

5 Escape tower
Be prepared – the rocket could blow up. In an emergency, this escape tower will blast off with its own smaller rockets and pull the command module away to safety.

APOLLO SPACECRAFT PARTS

As commander of this mission, make sure you are familiar with every part of your spacecraft.

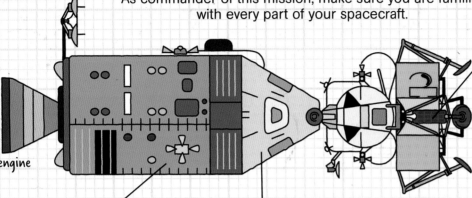

engine

Lunar module
To go down to the Moon's surface, you will travel in the lunar module. This part detaches itself from the rest of the spacecraft once you are in lunar orbit.

Service module
The service module holds the air and water for your trip. It also carries the fuel to power the engine and provides electricity.

Command module
Your home, the command module, contains the control panel and computer to guide the craft. Your food and medical kit are also stored here.

SPACE LINGO

CSM
The command module and service module, known together as the CSM, form the main part of the spacecraft.

How to ... reach Moon orbit

1. Blast-off

two rocket stages fall away

Blast-off is automatic. Lie back and try to relax as you feel your seat shake and shudder. Two stages of the rocket will drop away. You are now travelling at over 28,000 km per hour.

2. Orbit Earth

Orbit the Earth one-and-a-half times, then carry out a health check on your craft. The third stage of the rocket will fire and set you on course for the Moon at 38,000 km per hour.

3. Dock

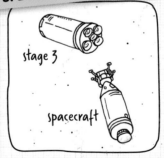

stage 3

spacecraft

After stage 3 of the rocket separates from your spacecraft, carefully guide the CSM back towards the stage so you can attach the lunar module stored inside. This is called docking.

4. Orbit Moon

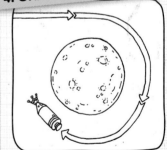

Cruise for 380,000 km, then pass around the far side of the Moon. You will lose radio contact with Earth for 45 minutes but don't panic! Fire the engine and enter Moon orbit.

MOON MISSION

It takes more than just three astronauts to reach the Moon! Planning a trip takes several years. You are part of a team that includes scientists, doctors and ground control staff. Everybody works together to make the journey as safe as they can.

This is the 'firing room' used during the Apollo missions. Staff sit behind rows of computers, launching the Saturn V rocket.

GROUND CONTROL

Staff on Earth will communicate with you throughout your mission. Launch Control will guide you through the take-off process, while Mission Control will monitor your progress through space and your journey home.

APOLLO FLIGHT PATH

Below are the flight paths that you will take to the Moon and back. Follow the routes and read about what will happen to your spacecraft at each stage.

Journey to the Moon

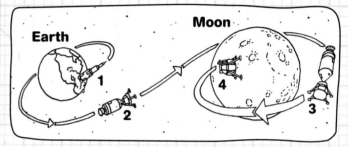

1 The Saturn V rocket lifts off from Earth.
2 The CSM detaches from stage 3 and heads for the Moon.
3 The spacecraft orbits the Moon.
4 The lunar module descends and lands on the Moon.

Journey to the Earth

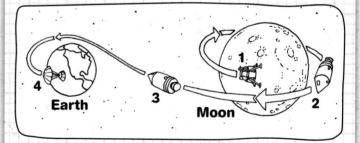

1 The lunar module launches from the Moon and joins the CSM.
2 The lunar crew dock with the CSM and orbit the Moon.
3 The CSM leaves the empty lunar module to return to Earth.
4 The command module splashes down into the sea.

READ YOUR MOON MAP

This map shows the nearside of the Moon, which is the part you can see from Earth and the side you will land on. Study it carefully, then look at the Moon through binoculars on a clear night to see if you can spot any of these features.

Sea of Rains
Large dark areas are called 'seas'. There is no water on the Moon, so these seas are dry. One of the largest seas is the Sea of Rains.

Where do I land?
There were six Apollo lunar landings. You're on the Apollo 11 mission – can you find your landing site? Check out nearby places to visit too.

Apennine Mountains
Mountain ranges stretch across the surface. The Apennines are home to the Moon's tallest peak.

Alpine Valley
There are valleys on the Moon, just like on Earth.

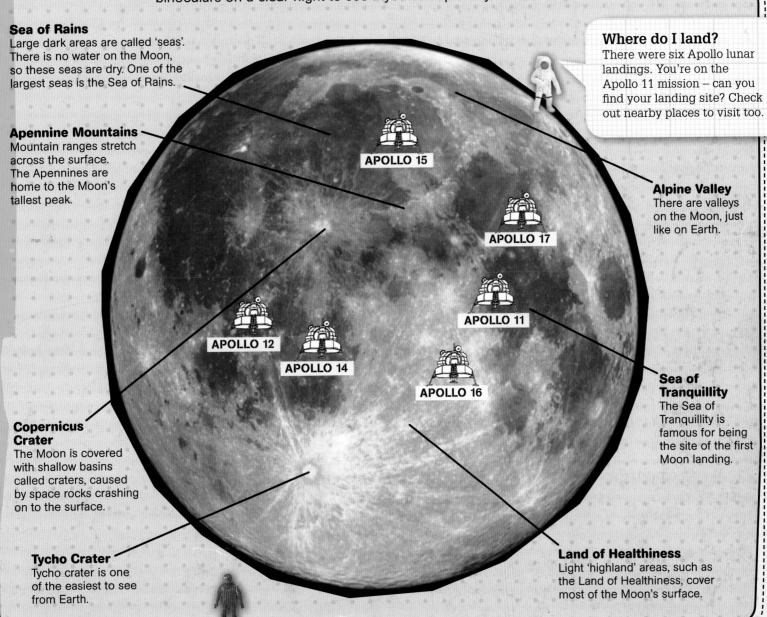

APOLLO 15

APOLLO 17

APOLLO 11

APOLLO 12

APOLLO 14

APOLLO 16

Sea of Tranquillity
The Sea of Tranquillity is famous for being the site of the first Moon landing.

Copernicus Crater
The Moon is covered with shallow basins called craters, caused by space rocks crashing on to the surface.

Tycho Crater
Tycho crater is one of the easiest to see from Earth.

Land of Healthiness
Light 'highland' areas, such as the Land of Healthiness, cover most of the Moon's surface.

MOON LANDING

You've flown through space for three days and the Moon is now a huge grey ball below. Climb inside the lunar module and guide it down to the surface carefully. Then take your first steps on an eerie silent world.

12:00

OPEN THE HATCH
Leave the lunar module and climb down the ladder, holding on to the rails. On the Moon there is little gravity – the force that pulls you to the ground – so you will feel light, even in a heavy spacesuit.

12:10

TAKE A MOONWALK
You won't be able to walk the way you do on Earth. Instead, you'll bounce about and it will be hard to keep your balance. Try hopping on both feet like a kangaroo or pushing off with your toes.

12:30

COLLECT SAMPLES
It's difficult to bend over, so use tools to collect rock and soil samples to be tested back on Earth. Watch out for the Moon dust! It's sharp and will stick to your spacesuit. It can easily wear away your boots and scratch your visor.

1:30 DO AN EXPERIMENT

Before you head back to base, set up a 'Moonquake' experiment. Leave the equipment behind so it can transmit data back to Earth about what is happening beneath the Moon's surface.

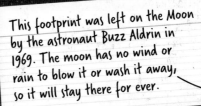

1:10 DRIVE THE LUNAR ROVER

Explore the Moon's plains, hills and valleys in a vehicle called a 'rover'. Push the hand controller forwards to drive and tilt it left or right to steer. You can reach a top speed of 18 km per hour in this battery-powered car.

This footprint was left on the Moon by the astronaut Buzz Aldrin in 1969. The moon has no wind or rain to blow it or wash it away, so it will stay there for ever.

ow to … fly the lunar module

Head down

lunar module

ou're sitting comfortably e flight controls. Separate the main spacecraft and e engine. You'll head with your back to the , looking at the stars.

2. Land

When the ground is visible, pinpoint your landing site on the computer. Fire your thrusters to slow down and steer away from craters. Cut the engine just before you touch down.

3. Head up

Only the top part of the lunar module lifts off from the Moon. The bottom acts as a launch pad. Set the controls to blow up the connecting bolts and fire the engine.

4. Dock

command module

Travel straight up at full speed, checking you're on course to meet up with the command module. Line up with small engine thrusts and connect the two spacecraft. Well done!

BACK TO EARTH

The command module is the only section of the Apollo spacecraft that comes back to Earth. The heat created while it speeds through the atmosphere means that parts of the outside get stripped away. The module is winched on board a ship after landing.

The journey home from the Moon is just as thrilling as the voyage out! Prepare for a red-hot trip through Earth's atmosphere and a sudden jolt as you splash down in the sea.

Ready to land?
You'll come back down to Earth inside the command module. Check out how it is designed to help keep you safe.

Heat shield
A heat shield protects you from the extreme temperatures caused by air in the atmosphere passing over the command module as you hurtle towards Earth.

Astronaut couches
You are strapped into a couch at the feet, waist and shoulders to keep you steady during the rocky ride.

Earth landing system
All the equipment you need to land safely (including eight parachutes!) is stored here in the nose cone.

Side hatch
After splashdown, you leave the command module through the side hatch.

Base
Landing on water at high speed is like hitting concrete, so a special crumple zone of steel ribs at the base helps to lessen the blow.

How to ... splash down

1. Re-entry

Before entering Earth's atmosphere, jettison the service module. Sit tight inside the command module as you fall at 40,000 km per hour. There will be a radio blackout.

2. Parachutes open

Your fall slows to 320 km per hour – too fast to land. About 7 km from Earth the heat shield around the nose cone ejects and a series of parachutes open.

3. Land on the water

You'll hit the water at about 20 km per hour. An inflating ring around the command module will keep you afloat and a radio will beep signals so that a boat can find you.

4. Lift to safety

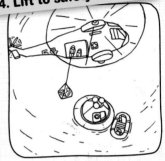

Climb out of the hatch and let a helicopter winch you to safety. You'll probably want to go straight home but you'll have to be checked over by doctors for the first few weeks.

RETURN TO THE MOON

For over 40 years no human has set foot on the Moon, but unmanned probes are still exploring Earth's neighbour. There are plans to return.

Altair lunar lander

crew lives in here

fuel tank

Grail-A

⭐ **UNMANNED PROBES**
In 2012 the Grail-A and -B probes were launched. They will collect data to help us understand what happens beneath the Moon's surface.

⭐ **LUNAR LANDER**
Altair is a spacecraft that is still being planned. It will be able to land humans on the Moon or other planets. The top will provide a home for the crew while the bottom will carry fuel and oxygen.

SHUTTLE LAUNCH

For your next flight, blast off in the Space Shuttle Atlantis and head for the International Space Station, which is orbiting the Earth. The team at launch control are on standby. This is going to be a thundering and scary ride!

Shuttle parts
The shuttle was the world's first reusable spacecraft. It lifted off the launch pad like a rocket and glided back to Earth like an aeroplane over 100 times between 1981 and 2011.

Orbiter
The crew travelled inside the orbiter, which could also hold a laboratory for carrying out experiments.

Rocket engines
The three main engines fired at lift-off but were not used for travelling in space.

Fuel tank
The largest part of the space shuttle was the fuel tank known as the ET (External Tank).

Rocket boosters
Two solid rocket boosters provided most of the power to lift the shuttle off the launch pad.

Atlantis
United States

3, 2, 1 ... LIFT-OFF!

Make sure you are strapped in as the onboard computers start the launch sequence.

1

Lift-off

Inside the orbiter, the onboard computers take over. The main engines fire and you hear a low rumble. Then the rocket boosters ignite. The shuttle lifts off.

2

Plus 2 minutes

As you head into the sky, you bounce about in your seat. It's a jerky ride! At about 45 km, the rocket boosters fall away. They will land in the sea to be collected and used again.

3

Plus 7 minutes

When you leave the Earth's atmosphere, the main engines power down. The giant fuel tank is now empty and falls away. It will burn up falling through the atmosphere back to Earth.

4

Plus 8.5 minutes

Smaller engines fire to place you first into a low orbit and then into a higher orbit. Inside the shuttle, everything is quiet. Your space mission is under way.

WOW FACTS

☞ The Space Shuttle programme took a total of 357 people into space, including astronauts, scientists and teachers.

☞ During the programme, the shuttles travelled over half-a-billion miles. That's further than to planet Jupiter!

☞ The orbiter is 37 m long, over three times the length of a school bus! It weighs more than 13 elephants.

It's a 5 km walk for the astronauts from the main building to the launch pad, so they take the bus! A huge crowd cheers them on as they head off on their historic journey.

SPACE STATION

A space station is both a base and a home in space. Spacecraft can dock with it so that astronauts can climb on board. You'll spend six months living on the International Space Station (ISS). This is the biggest and most expensive space station ever built.

BUILDING THE ISS

Begun in 1998, the International Space Station was built by 16 countries, including Russia, the USA and Japan. The space shuttle carried up the different parts, which were put together high above the Earth.

FAST FACTS

The International Space Station ...

✔ is nearly the length of a football pitch and over twice as wide.

✔ travels round the Earth at a speed of 480 km per minute.

✔ sits 385 km high above Earth.

✔ carries a crew of six people.

Solar panels
The huge solar panels provide electricity for the space station. Each pair is longer than the wingspan of a jumbo jet.

To connect with the ISS, the space shuttle stopped about 50 m away from the docking port. When the go-ahead was given, the pilot closed in, watching a specially designed target on a computer screen. It was a skilful operation to line up the two craft.

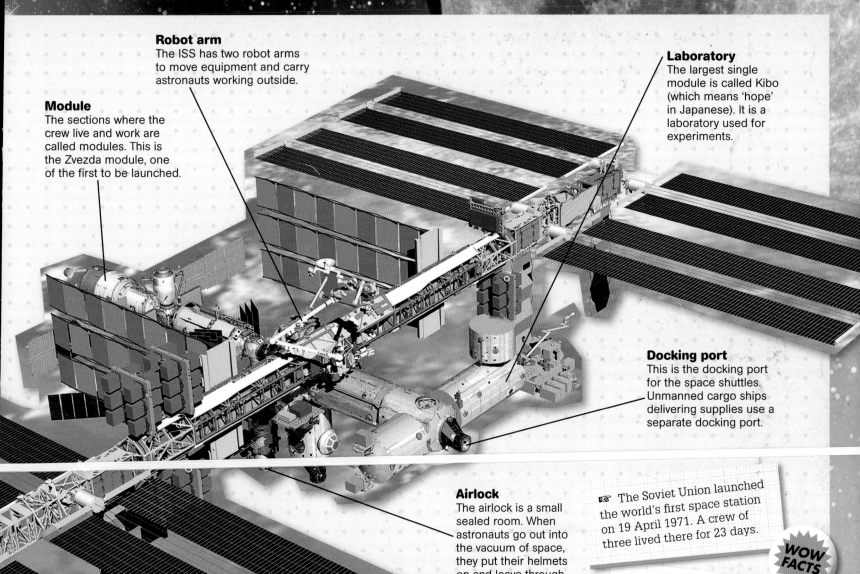

Robot arm
The ISS has two robot arms to move equipment and carry astronauts working outside.

Module
The sections where the crew live and work are called modules. This is the Zvezda module, one of the first to be launched.

Laboratory
The largest single module is called Kibo (which means 'hope' in Japanese). It is a laboratory used for experiments.

Docking port
This is the docking port for the space shuttles. Unmanned cargo ships delivering supplies use a separate docking port.

Airlock
The airlock is a small sealed room. When astronauts go out into the vacuum of space, they put their helmets on and leave through the airlock.

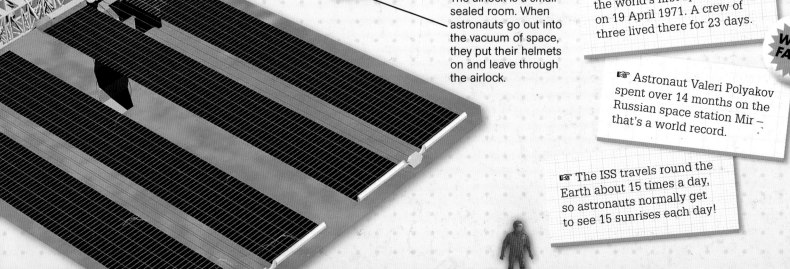

☞ The Soviet Union launched the world's first space station on 19 April 1971. A crew of three lived there for 23 days.

WOW FACTS

☞ Astronaut Valeri Polyakov spent over 14 months on the Russian space station Mir – that's a world record.

☞ The ISS travels round the Earth about 15 times a day, so astronauts normally get to see 15 sunrises each day!

21

SPACEWALK

When an astronaut does jobs outside a spacecraft, such as making repairs or moving equipment, it's called a spacewalk. Leaving the spacecraft is exciting but dangerous! Are you ready to go outside the space station?

2 PICK UP YOUR TOOLS

Take your tools with you. Doing delicate jobs can be tricky because you have to wear thick gloves. Space tools often have bigger handles than the tools used on Earth so that they are easier to hold.

1 OPEN THE HATCH

First sleep in the airlock overnight to get your body ready for the low pressure in space. Put on your spacesuit, then open the hatch and climb outside. Use the handrails to move about.

SPACE LINGO

EVA
A spacewalk is also known as an EVA. This stands for Extra Vehicular Activity – that's an activity outside your spacecraft.

3 MAKE REPAIRS

During a spacewalk you are attached to the space station by thin, strong wires. This means you can move about without floating off! Often you work with another astronaut. Concentrate hard and carry out your repairs.

4

WORK ON THE ROBOT ARM
Finally, head to the robot arm and clamp your feet on to the platform. Reduced gravity means objects feel much lighter in space, so moving a large piece of equipment like this isn't quite as difficult as it looks. Well done!

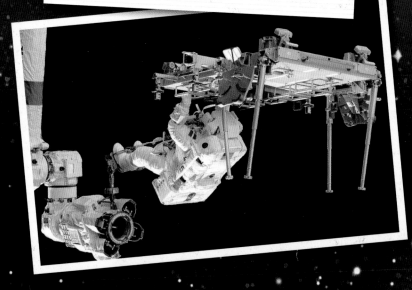

MMU

In 1984, on three space shuttle missions, astronauts used an MMU (Manned Manoeuvring Unit) for spacewalks. This 'flying armchair' with controls allowed them to move about and work freely.

How to ... live in space

1. Washing

Daily life in space is different from life on Earth. On a space station, there are no showers because water will not fall to the floor. Instead, astronauts wash themselves with a soapy towel.

2. Eating

Food comes in sealed packets. Much of it is freeze-dried and needs to be mixed with water and heated up. Astronauts drink through a tube to stop blobs of liquid floating away.

3. Exercising

Less gravity means your muscles and bones waste away in space, so it's really important to keep fit. Astronauts exercise every day on treadmills and exercise bikes. They also lift weights.

4. Sleeping

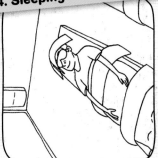

There is no right way up so astronauts can sleep anywhere. Instead of using a bed, they usually climb into a sleeping bag that is strapped to the wall or floor so they don't float off.

SHUTTLE AT WORK

Before you head home, you're going to get more familiar with the parts of a space shuttle orbiter and repair a space telescope. Inside the orbiter, there is a huge payload bay for transporting cargo and other useful equipment.

Cabin
The commander and crew lived in the cabin. The flight deck was on top, with the living quarters below.

Cargo
This orbiter was carrying a module to add to the International Space Station. It could also carry satellites to launch into orbit.

Payload bay
The payload bay was 18 m long. In space, the doors were kept open to let heat escape.

Heat tiles
Thousands of heat tiles protected the orbiter. When re-entering the Earth's atmosphere, temperatures could reach 1,357°C!

Wing flaps
These flaps on the edges of the wings moved up and down to help control descent and landing.

Thrusters
The thrusters allowed the craft to turn and change direction in space.

Atlantis

Did you know?
Spacelab, a reusable laboratory, was carried in the payload bay on 22 missions so astronauts could complete science experiments.

Repairing a space telescope was a tough task. First the shuttle had to capture the telescope with its robot arm. Then astronauts performed a spacewalk to fix the telescope. Here, the Hubble Space Telescope, which observes distant galaxies, is about to be serviced.

The flight deck contains all the computers to programme the shuttle, as well as a communication system so that you can speak to Mission Control. Before flying the shuttle for real, astronauts practise in a simulator such as this one.

TIME TO TOUCH DOWN
Keep calm, strap yourself in and prepare for touchdown. Your mission is complete!

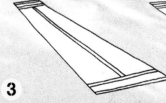

1

4 hours to go ...
You're circling the Earth at a height of 320 km. Prepare the onboard computers for re-entry and landing. Then close the payload bay doors.

2

2 hours ...
When you hit Earth's atmosphere, the engines must be off. Use the steering thrusters to control the orbiter. Burn up your leftover fuel.

3

5 minutes ...
You're now flying the orbiter like an aeroplane – but travelling at over 1,300 km per hour and closing in on the runway! Pull up the nose to slow down.

4

0 minutes
Lower the wheels and hit the runway. Then start to break. A parachute will open behind you to help you stop. Congratulations!

ASTRONAUT SCHOOL

SPACE MAP

Flying a spacecraft is an awesome experience but you need to know where you are going! In this lesson, learn about the planets that make up our solar system and discover where you can find them.

JUPITER
What: gas planet
Distance from Earth: 624.4 million km
Jupiter is the biggest of all the planets. Over 1,000 Earths could fit inside it!

MERCURY
What: rocky planet
Distance from Earth: 91.7 million km
Mercury is the smallest planet and the closest to the Sun.

The Moon isn't a planet at all! It's a natural satellite that circles the Earth.

MARS
What: rocky planet
Distance from Earth: 78.3 million km
Mars is the planet most like Earth. There may once have been water on its surface.

EARTH
What: rocky planet
Earth is the only planet where we know there is life.

VENUS
What: rocky planet
Distance from Earth: 41.4 million km
Venus is the hottest planet with temperatures reaching over 400˚C.

START HERE

Can you find it?

Q: You're launching a probe to Jupiter. How many planets is it away from Earth? Which planets does it orbit between?

A: Jupiter is two planets away from Earth. It orbits between Mars and Saturn.

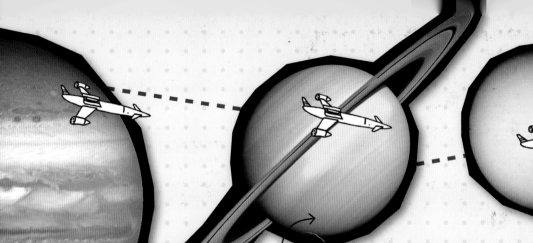

⭐ URANUS
What: gas planet
Distance from Earth:
2.7 billion km
Uranus is so far away from the Sun that one orbit takes 84 Earth years!

⭐ SATURN
What: gas planet
Distance from Earth:
1.2 billion km
Saturn, with its spectacular rings, is the most distant planet we can see without a telescope.

⭐ NEPTUNE
What: gas planet
Distance from Earth:
4.3 billion km
Neptune has poisonous blue clouds and the fastest winds in the solar system.

⭐ PLUTO
What: dwarf planet
Distance from Earth:
4.4–7.4 billion km
Pluto is dark, ice-cold and rocky. Would you want to fly there?

Our solar system

The solar system is the name given to the Sun and all the other objects in space that travel round it. There are nine planets including Pluto, which is so small that it is called a dwarf planet.

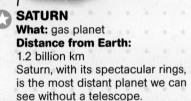

asteroid belt

Sun

Planets
1 Mercury
2 Venus
3 Earth
4 Mars
5 Jupiter
6 Saturn
7 Uranus
8 Neptune
9 Pluto

Lumps of rock, called asteroids, travel through space. They were formed millions of years ago from leftover bits of planets. A belt of asteroids circles the Sun between Mars and Jupiter.

27

DESTINATION MARS

Flying humans to Mars is still a dream but robot craft have already explored this red planet's rocky surface. The latest spacecraft to touch down was Curiosity, a rover the size of a large car. It reached Mars on 6 August 2012.

Crash or land?

It took over eight months for Curiosity to fly to Mars. The trip had passed smoothly but would the spacecraft survive its hair-raising landing? Join the live transmission!

1

INTO THE ATMOSPHERE
The metal pod carrying Curiosity blasts into the Martian atmosphere. The heat shield protecting the rover gets as hot as the surface of the Sun!

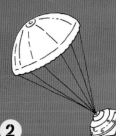

2

PARACHUTE OPEN
The pod is travelling at more than 1,600 km per hour. If it carries on like this it will crash! A giant parachute opens to slow down the craft.

Curiosity in action

Curiosity's mission is to investigate the Martian soil and climate to see if conditions are right for tiny forms of life. The rover drives around scooping up rocks and soil, which it analyses inside its onboard lab. It also takes photographs.

camera mast with seven 'eyes'

antenna beams back pictures and data to Earth

robotic arm collects rocks and soil

rock crusher in here

lab for testing samples in here

Curiosity

3
HEAT SHIELD OFF
Inside the pod, there is radar equipment to pinpoint the landing site. The heat shield will block the radar, so it drops away.

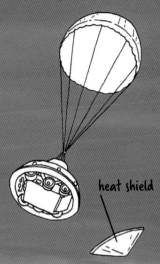

heat shield

4
PARACHUTE OFF
The pod is still going too fast to land. The parachute and top of the pod break away leaving rocket engines to control Curiosity's descent.

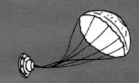
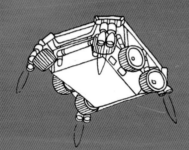

5
SKY CRANE
But there's another complication! If Curiosity gets too near the ground, the firing engines will create a dust cloud that could damage the rover. So instead, a sky crane lowers Curiosity.

sky crane

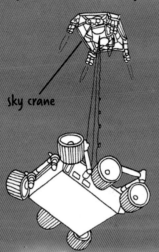

SPACE LINGO

MSL
MSL is the name of the mission. It stands for Mars Science Laboratory. It's called this because Curiosity is a science lab on wheels!

6
TOUCHDOWN
Curiosity touches down but the danger still isn't over. The sky crane is heading towards the rover. The wires snap automatically and the sky crane shoots off. Mission accomplished!

Did you know?
Scientists described Curiosity's seven-minute descent to Mars as 'seven minutes of terror'. This was because there was nothing they could do if something went wrong!

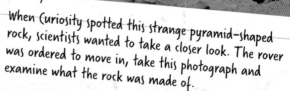

When Curiosity spotted this strange pyramid-shaped rock, scientists wanted to take a closer look. The rover was ordered to move in, take this photograph and examine what the rock was made of.

ROBOT CRAFT

Scientists launch all kinds of unmanned craft into space to do all kinds of jobs. Let's find out how these robot vehicles work.

heat shields protect equipment from the Sun's rays

telescope collects data

James Webb

the spacecraft 'bus' is the nerve centre, it powers and controls the satellite

CARGO SHIP

This 2011 cargo ship delivered food, fuel, water and equipment to astronauts on the International Space Station. Once the supplies were unloaded, the spacecraft headed back into the Earth's atmosphere and burned up.

HTV-3

SPACE TELESCOPE

The James Webb space telescope is due to be launched in 2018. Like the Hubble Space Telescope, it will look at distant stars and galaxies to help us find out how the universe was formed.

WOW FACTS

☞ Before a cargo ship leaves a space station, it is loaded up with waste. It's a bit like a giant space dustbin!

Robonaut II isn't a spacecraft but he's definitely a robot! He lives on the International Space Station and helps the astronauts with their jobs. Robonaut has no legs, so he is screwed on to a pole to work.

Galileo

SPACE PROBE

The Galileo spacecraft was an unmanned long-distance explorer that dropped a probe into the thick swirling clouds around the planet Jupiter. The spacecraft also flew past Io, Jupiter's closest moon, where it observed giant erupting volcanoes. Its 14-year mission ended in 2003.

Jupiter

GALILEO FIRSTS

Galileo was the first spacecraft to …

✔ orbit the planet Jupiter and study its atmosphere.

✔ fly close up to an asteroid.

✔ discover that some asteroids have their own moons.

✔ observe a comet colliding with another planet.

How to ... release Galileo's probe

1. Into space

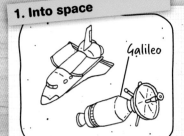

Galileo

On 18 October 1989, the Galileo spacecraft was launched from the payload bay of the Space Shuttle Atlantis. This was the start of a flight to Jupiter lasting nearly six years.

2. On its way

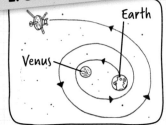

Earth

Venus

Instead of travelling straight there, Galileo cruised twice around Venus and the Earth. It took energy from these planets' gravity to help power it to its destination.

3. Nearly there

It cruised through the solar system, taking the first detailed photos of Gaspra and Ida – two asteroids. By the time it got close to Jupiter, it had travelled over 4.6 billion km.

4. Drop the probe

The spacecraft released its probe into Jupiter's poisonous atmosphere. Speeding down at 170,500 km per hour, the probe transmitted data back to Earth before eventually burning up.

SPACEPLANE

Are you ready to rocket to the edge of space in the world's first spaceplane for tourists? You'll be in the cockpit of SpaceShip Two, taking passengers into zero gravity. Here the pull of the Earth disappears and everyone on board will feel completely weightless.

To get into the sky, SpaceShip Two hitches a ride on WhiteKnight Two, a specially designed launcher. WhiteKnight Two takes off like a normal aeroplane and SpaceShip Two sits beneath the launcher in the middle.

WhiteKnight Two

SpaceShip Two

WOW FACTS

☞ For part of the journey, SpaceShip Two travels at 3,600 km per hour – three times faster than the speed of sound!

☞ On a test flight for an earlier version of SpaceShip Two, the plane spun round and round as it nosedived to Earth. Brave pilots landed it safely.

☞ From take-off to landing, the experience lasts two-and-a-half hours, with five minutes spent floating weightless in space.

Ride of a lifetime
As captain, you must keep calm and concentrate hard, but don't forget to enjoy the ride! When you reach space, watch the sky fade from blue to black. The cockpit will fall silent. Look out of the window to see the curve of our blue planet below.

How to ... reach zero gravity

1. The drop

WhiteKnight Two will release your spaceship at a height of 15 km. As you drop and glide in the sky for a few seconds, check all the controls and get ready for the astonishing ride.

2. Blast-off

Now fire up the rocket engines. Concentrate as you are thrown back against your seat and zoom straight up towards space. You are on your way to zero gravity.

3. Engines off

When you reach a height of about 70 km, you are in space and the rocket engine shuts down. Your passengers will float out of their seats and feel weightless.

4. The glide

Head back down, keeping the spaceship steady as you pick up speed. When you start to slow down, flip the switch to aeroplane mode. Glide to Earth and land on the runway.

Robot plane

There are robot spaceplanes in development (such as the X-37B) that will work without a pilot. It will be possible to relaunch them on a rocket.

X-37B

The X-37B is about one-quarter of the size of a shuttle, and it can be launched on top of a rocket. An outer case protects the robot plane from the pressure and heat of take-off, then it falls away.

⭐ **TOP SECRET**
The X-37B looks a lot like the space shuttle's orbiter. It has an extending robot arm for jobs such as mending and refuelling satellites. The plane has made several top secret test flights and remained in orbit for over a year.

FUTURE TRAVEL

One day, astronauts are likely to return to the Moon. They may build colonies on Mars or even fly to other, more distant, planets. How might they get there? What might life be like? Take a look and decide if you want to join the team.

solar panels

Orion

⭐ SPACECRAFT TO THE MOON

The Orion MPCV (Multi-Purpose Crew Vehicle) is being developed for missions to the Moon, Mars and large asteroids. It will have room for a crew of four astronauts.

engine

Skylon

payload bay

fuel tank inside body

streamlined shape

⭐ FUTURE SPACESHIP

Skylon is a design for a robot spaceplane but there are plans to develop it so that it could carry a captain and passengers too. The technology used to build Skylon could help us to design a spaceship for long-distance space travel.

Did you know?

Skylon has an incredible air-breathing engine that takes oxygen from outside the plane. This will allow it to travel into space at lightning speed without the need for huge fuel tanks.

IMAGINE THIS!

Future astronauts may spend many years living and working in space. They may even stay and raise their families there permanently.

MOON BASE

There are plans to build a scientific base on the Moon. From here astronauts could conduct long-term experiments. The base could also serve as a refuelling stop for spacecraft on their way to other planets.

MARS MOBILE HOME

On Mars, a motorhome, equipped with oxygen and other supplies would allow astronauts to drive around and investigate the planet's surface. Could Mars be a place for humans to settle?

SPACE HOTEL

Would you like to live and work on a space station? As technology improves, space stations will probably become bigger and more comfortable. They may even turn into hotels where your friends and family can take a relaxing holiday!

ASTEROID NEWS

In the future, asteroids may be big news. Space scientists are trying to learn more about them.

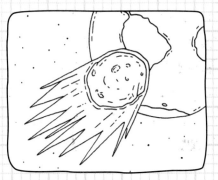

Crashing to Earth

It's unlikely, but a huge asteroid could crash to Earth. Scientists are investigating how a spacecraft might push asteroids out of the Earth's path to keep us safe.

Mining for minerals

Companies are working on the technology to mine asteroids. One day, a spacecraft could dock with an asteroid and drill a hole into its surface to extract its minerals.

SPACE ROCKETS

People have built fireworks and rockets since ancient times but only in the 1940s did rockets become large and powerful enough to reach space. A rocket has sections called stages.

SOYUZ

Built: Soviet Union (later Russia)
Height: up to 54.3 m
Thrust*: 1.1 million lb
Number of stages: 3
First launch: 1957
Launches: about 1,500 in total

⭐ Soyuz rockets have flown into space more times than any other type of rocket. This modern Soyuz-FG carries cargo and people to the International Space Station.

SATURN V

MOST POWERFUL

Built: USA
Height: 110.6 m
Thrust: 7.5 million lb
Number of stages: 3
First launch: 1967
Launches: 13 in total

⭐ This is the world's most famous rocket. From 1967 to 1972, it took 24 people to the Moon. It also launched the first space station, Skylab.

DELTA IV HEAVY

Built: USA
Height: up to 72 m
Thrust: 2.2 million lb
Number of stages: 2
First launch: 2004
Launches: about 2 a year

⭐ Delta IV Heavy is the largest rocket in the Delta family. It launches satellites into orbit with the help of two huge booster rockets strapped to the main body.

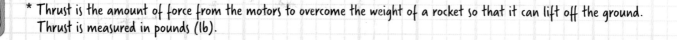

* Thrust is the amount of force from the motors to overcome the weight of a rocket so that it can lift off the ground. Thrust is measured in pounds (lb).

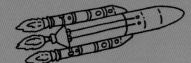

ARIANE 5

Built: Europe
Height: up to 52 m
Thrust: 3 million lb
Number of stages: 2
First launch: 2002
Launches: about 8 a year

⭐ Ariane 5's first launch ended with the rocket exploding after 37 seconds but it has worked well since. It is large enough to carry two satellites in its payload bay.

ATLAS 5

Built: USA
Height: 58.3 m
Thrust: 5.3 million lb
Number of stages: 2
First launch: 2002
Launches: about 5 a year

⭐ This satellite launcher has an almost perfect success rate. Its specially designed engines allow it to 'park' in orbit, so it can easily release its load.

SPACED OUT!
The Falcon 9 rocket was built by a billionaire with an interest in space. He has also built a new spacecraft called Dragon. Maybe one day you will too!

FALCON 9

Built: USA
Height: 54 m
Thrust: 1.1 million lb
Number of stages: 2
First launch: 2010
Launches: about 8 a year

⭐ Falcon 9 is a very advanced rocket. In 2012, it made history by delivering Dragon – the first privately owned spacecraft – to the International Space Station.

In 1969, American Buzz Aldrin became the second astronaut to set foot on the Moon. He travelled as part of a crew of three people in the Saturn V rocket on the Apollo II mission. He spent several hours on the Moon's surface, collecting lunar rocks to bring back to Earth.

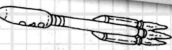

SATELLITES

Artificial or human-made, satellites are unmanned spacecraft that circle the Earth. They do everything from studying the weather to sending signals to mobile phones and TV stations.

SPUTNIK 1

Built: Soviet Union
Use: to study Earth's atmosphere
Size: as big as a beach ball
Orbits*: 15 a day
Launch date: 4 October 1957
Launch vehicle: Sputnik rocket

⭐ Sputnik 1 was the first artificial satellite launched into space. It beeped signals from its four wire antennae back to Earth for 22 days before its batteries ran out.

RADARSAT-2

Built: Canada
Use: to study Earth's surface
Size: as long as a bus
Orbits: 14 a day
Launch date: 14 December 2007
Launch vehicle: Soyuz rocket

⭐ This is one of many different Earth-watching satellites. As well as mapping out land use, Radarsat-2 detects icebergs and sea pollution.

GPS III

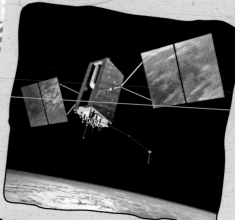

Built: USA
Use: for navigation
Size: as long as a bus
Orbits: 2 a day
Launch date: planned for 2014
Launch vehicle: Atlas rocket

⭐ GPS stands for Global Positioning System. Satnav equipment in cars, which helps you find the way with an electronic map, makes use of lots of GPS satellites.

* The number of orbits tells you how many times the satellite goes around the Earth in one day.

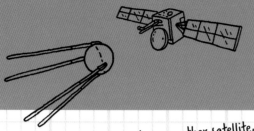

This photograph, taken by a weather satellite, shows a hurricane developing over the coast of North America. By tracking cloud formations, weather satellites can give us advance warning of storms, helping to save lives.

B-SAT 2A

Built: Japan
Use: for broadcasting TV
Size: as long as a bus
Orbits: 1 a day
Launch date: 8 March 2001
Launch vehicle: Ariane rocket

⭐ A broadcast satellite such as this allows you to watch digital TV programmes from all over the world. The satellite beams the signal to your rooftop dish.

LARGEST

INTELSAT 22

Built: UK
Use: for wireless communication
Size: as long as two buses
Orbits: 1 a day
Launch date: 25 March 2012
Launch vehicle: Proton rocket

⭐ This communication satellite provides internet and phone services so that you can talk to people on the other side of the world. Solar panels power it in space.

METEOSAT-1

Built: Europe
Use: for weather forecasts
Size: as tall as a room in a house
Orbits: 1 a day
Launch date: 23 November 1977
Launch vehicle: Delta rocket

⭐ Weather satellites, such as Meteosat-1, watch cloud patterns and measure wind strength. They also record the temperature of the land, sea and air.

SPACED OUT!
There are about 4,500 satellites floating in space. Around 500 of these satellites are working — the rest are space junk!

SPACE SHUTTLES

Between 1981 and 2011, the US Space Shuttle programme flew 135 missions. There were five shuttle orbiters that went to space and one test vehicle.

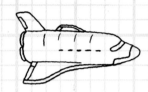

ENTERPRISE

shuttle

First flight: 15 February 1977 (test)
Last flight: 27 April 2012
Missions: none
Time in space: airborne only
Orbits: none
Satellites launched: none

⭐ Enterprise was the first orbiter to be built. It had no engines or heat shield, and was carried into the sky on the back of a jumbo jet for flight and landing tests.

COLUMBIA

First flight: 12 April 1981
Last flight: 16 January 2003
Missions: 28
Time in space: 300 days
Orbits: 4,808
Satellites launched: 8

⭐ Columbia completed the first shuttle mission, lasting just over two days. On 16 January 2003, Columbia exploded while re-entering Earth's atmosphere.

CHALLENGER

First flight: 4 April 1983
Last flight: 28 January 1986
Missions: 10
Time in space: 62 days
Orbits: 995
Satellites launched: 10

⭐ Astronauts performed their first shuttle spacewalk on a Challenger mission. Sadly, in 1986, Challenger exploded 73 seconds after launch.

DISCOVERY

First flight: 30 August 1984
Last flight: 24 February 2011
Missions: 39
Time in space: 365 days
Orbits: 5,830
Satellites launched: 31

⭐ Discovery launched the Hubble Space Telescope as well as many satellites. It also docked with the International Space Station more times than any other orbiter.

ATLANTIS

First flight: 3 October 1985
Last flight: 8 July 2011
Missions: 33
Time in space: 306 days
Orbits: 4,848
Satellites launched: 14

⭐ Atlantis flew the last ever shuttle mission. It took equipment up to the International Space station, remaining in orbit for just over two weeks.

SPACED OUT!

A space shuttle orbiter travels at about 28,000 km per hour as it circles Earth — over 25 times faster than the speed of sound!

ENDEAVOUR

First flight: 7 May 1992
Last flight: 7 May 2011
Missions: 25
Time in space: 296 days
Orbits: 4,671
Satellites launched: 3

⭐ US school students named Endeavour as part of a national competition. On several of its missions astronauts carried out experiments in Spacelab.

In the early days of space travel, most astronauts were men; however, today many women train to be astronauts. Over 50 female astronauts flew in the space shuttles, including Naoko Yamazaki from Japan.

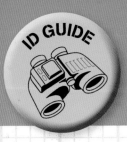
SPACE PROBES

Since the 1950s, scientists have been developing robot craft, called space probes, to study objects in our solar system. These craft beam back pictures and information to Earth.

IKAROS

Built: Japan
Launch: 21 May 2010
Mass: 315 kg
Studies: Venus
Mission length: over 2 years
In operation: yes

⭐ Ikaros is the first space probe to use solar sails and the Sun's light to power it through space, spinning as it travels. It is now on its way to the far side of the Sun.

LUNA 16

Built: Soviet Union
Launch: 12 September 1970
Mass: 5,600 kg
Studies: Moon
Mission length: 12 days
In operation: no

⭐ Between 1959 and 1976, the Soviet Union launched 24 Luna space probes to study the Moon. Luna 16 was the first robotic probe to return soil samples to Earth.

SOHO

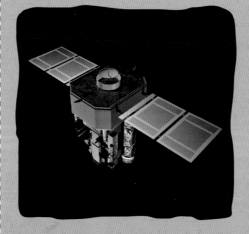

Built: Europe
Launch: 2 December 1995
Mass: 1,850 kg
Studies: Sun and space weather
Mission length: over 16 years
In operation: yes

⭐ SOHO (Solar and Heliospheric Observatory) has taught us lots about how space storms and solar flares around the Sun could affect us on Earth.

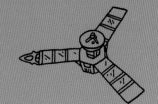

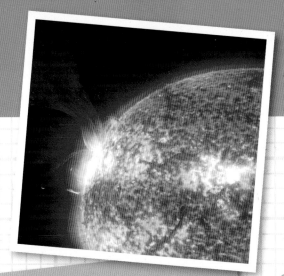

SOHO captured this image of a solar flare erupting from the Sun. A solar flare happens when a massive amount of the Sun's energy is suddenly released. The effect can be so strong that it may trigger space storms that knock out electrical power lines on Earth.

JUNO

Built: USA
Launch: 5 August 2011
Mass: 3,625 kg
Studies: Jupiter
Mission length: 6 years (planned)
In operation: yes

⭐ Scientists are hopeful that Juno will reach Jupiter in 2016, five years after launch. It will search for clues about how this enormous gas planet was formed.

CASSINI

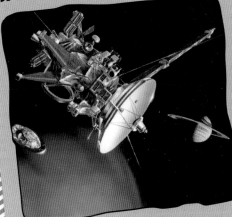

Built: USA and Europe
Launch: 5 October 1997
Mass: 2,525 kg
Studies: Saturn and its moons
Mission length: over 14 years
In operation: yes

⭐ The Cassini mission included a visit to Titan, Saturn's largest moon. Cassini successfully released a small probe, called Huygens, into Titan's thick orange gas clouds.

VOYAGER 1

LONGEST MISSION

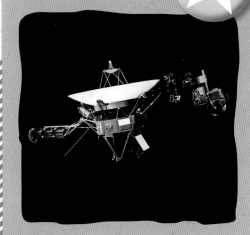

Built: USA
Launch: 5 September 1977
Mass: 720 kg
Studies: Jupiter and Saturn
Mission length: over 34 years
In operation: yes

⭐ Voyager 1 and 2 were identical spacecraft that flew to the gas planets Jupiter, Saturn, Uranus and Neptune to study their atmosphere and moons.

SPACED OUT!

Voyager 1 is now heading out of our solar system deep into interstellar space. It carries a message on a disc for any alien life forms it might meet!

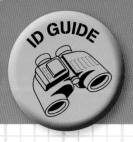

LANDERS & ROVERS

Space scientists on earth can explore the surface of Mars and the Moon with robot landers and rovers. These vehicles usually carry scientific tools and cameras.

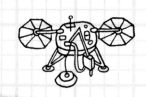

SURVEYOR 1

Built: USA
Launched by: Atlas-Centaur rocket
Landed: 2 June 1966
Mass: 290 kg
Explores: Moon
Mission length: 12 days

⭐ The Surveyor landers helped prepare for the manned Apollo missions. In 1966, Surveyor 1 took photos of the Moon's surface and transmitted them back to Earth.

HEAVIEST

LUNOKHOD 1

Built: Soviet Union
Launched by: Proton rocket
Landed: 17 November 1970
Mass: 755 kg
Explores: Moon
Mission length: 322 days

⭐ Lunokhod 1 was the first successful lunar rover. It moved around collecting information while controlled by scientists on Earth. Its name means 'Moon walker'.

PHOENIX LANDER

Built: USA
Launched by: Delta rocket
Landed: 25 May 2008
Mass: 350 kg
Explores: Mars
Mission length: 160 days

⭐ The Phoenix spacecraft landed on Mars at the polar caps. It used its robot arm to dig into the ground and look for signs of water and tiny forms of life.

SOJOURNER

Built: USA
Launched by: Delta rocket
Landed: 4 July 1997
Mass: 10.5 kg
Explores: Mars
Mission length: 84 days

⭐ The Sojourner rover was part of the Mars Pathfinder mission. It analysed rocks and studied the Martian weather. It was about the size of a microwave oven.

Sojourner was delivered to Mars by a lander. It rolled down a platform on to the planet's surface and began exploring nearby rocks. This photo was taken by the camera on the lander.

LUNAR ROVERS

Built: USA
Launched by: Saturn V rocket
Landed: 1971, 1972 (3 missions)
Mass: 210 kg
Explores: Moon
Mission length: 3 days

⭐ Astronauts drove the 'moon buggy' on the last three Apollo missions. It was a quick way to get around. All three rovers remain on the Moon.

INSIGHT

Built: USA and Europe
Launched by: not yet announced
Landing: 2016 (planned)
Mass: 350 kg
Explores: Mars
Mission length: about 2 years

⭐ InSight will look beneath the surface of Mars. It will measure 'Marsquakes' and investigate the planet's rocky core to help find out how Mars formed.

SPACE QUIZ

Put yourself in the hot seat and take this crazy intergalactic quiz! The answers are at the side of the page. Keep on trying until you get them all right!

2

How did the Apollo astronauts descend to the Moon's surface?

a) in the lunar module
b) in the lunar rover
c) in a sky crane

1

What is the biggest rocket ever built?

a) Soyuz
b) Saturn V
c) Delta IV Heavy

3

If you dropped a hammer and a feather on the Moon at the same time, what would happen?

a) the feather would land first
b) they would land at the same time
c) the hammer would land first

4

Roughly how many times a day does the International Space Station travel round the Earth?

a) once
b) 15 times
c) 100 times

5

If you put an ice cube into the fuel tank of a space shuttle, how long would it take to melt?

a) 8.5 seconds
b) 8.5 minutes
c) 8.5 years

6

Which of these foods is not on the menu at the International Space Station?

a) hamburgers – too greasy
b) baked potatoes – they explode in space
c) bread – crumbs can damage equipment

7

What could happen to you if you fell into a black hole? You might …

a) stretch out like spaghetti
b) turn bright green
c) shrink to the size of a bean

10

How much of the dust in your bedroom might come from space?

a) none
b) one-third
c) all of it

11

What's the largest piece of space junk that ever fell to Earth?

a) a space station
b) a rocket
c) a space shuttle

12

When a large star explodes it's called a supernova. How much energy does a supernova release? The same as ...

a) 10 stars
b) 10 million stars
c) 100 billion stars

9

How many pieces of space junk – that's bits of old spacecraft, rocket and satellite – are there floating about up there?

a) 50 pieces
b) 500 pieces
c) 500,000 pieces

8

Which of these is not the name of an asteroid?

a) Gaspra
b) Platypus
c) Ida

How did you score?

0–5 Whoops! Keep training and learning about space and you'll get there in the end.

6–9 Well done! You've blasted off the launch pad.

10–12 Top marks! You're a first-rate space pilot rocketing through the galaxy!

Answers
1b, 2a, 3b, 4b, 5c, 6c, 7a, 8b, 9c, 10b, 11a, 12c

SPACE ACADEMY CERTIFICATE
CONGRATULATIONS!

You have now completed your astronaut training and been awarded your Commander certificate and badge. Happy space flights!

Signed

David Baker

Head of Mission Control

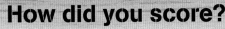

INDEX

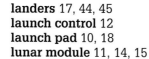

SPACECRAFT NAMES

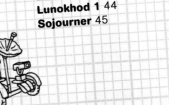